Derek Williams and Jacqui

WHAT'S WHAT IN THE BIBLE

CONTENTS

Homes and Houses

THE HOUSEHOLD

In Bible times, the word for "house" is also often used for household – the family.

God's people are called "God's household" or family.

Sometimes the Temple is called "God's house", meaning the place where he is honored.

ROMAN HOUSES

In larger Roman cities there were blocks of flats several floors high, housing many families. The flats were dark and smelly and could easily catch fire. They had no proper water supply, drainage or heating.

Rich Romans lived in spacious villas, often built around an atrium, a central courtyard open to the sky. Rain fell through the opening and filled a pool which could be used for washing or collecting drinking water. Around the atrium might be a peristyle, a covered walkway with the roof supported by pillars.

Luxury villas had mosaics on the floors and murals on the walls. Rich Roman families had many slaves, who lived in the house.

Many people in the early Bible stories were nomads. They lived in tents, moving from place to place to find fresh grass and water for their animals. As people settled in villages and towns, they began to live in simple houses. Most people had few possessions.

Living in tents

- **Tents** Made of animal skins or woven goats' hair, the cloth was hung over a wooden frame and held down with ropes and pegs hammered into the ground. In the heat of the day, the sides were rolled up. When Abraham was told by three visitors that he would have a son, Sarah listened behind the curtain.
- **The tent of meeting** The Israelites lived in tents when they left Egypt. Even their Temple was a tent called the tabernacle or tent of meeting, and contained an altar for sacrifice and the Covenant Box.

Simple houses

- **Building materials** Simple one-room houses, about 9 feet square, were made out of clay bricks or stone. Houses had to be built on solid rock.
- **Flat roof** The roof was made of beams of wood laid across the walls. The space between them was filled with branches and coated with mud plaster pressed down by a heavy roller. The roof was often used as an upstairs room in summer, with a canopy made from branches, cloth or animal skins to give shade. By law there had to be a parapet to stop people falling off.

Abraham and Sarah lived in tents.

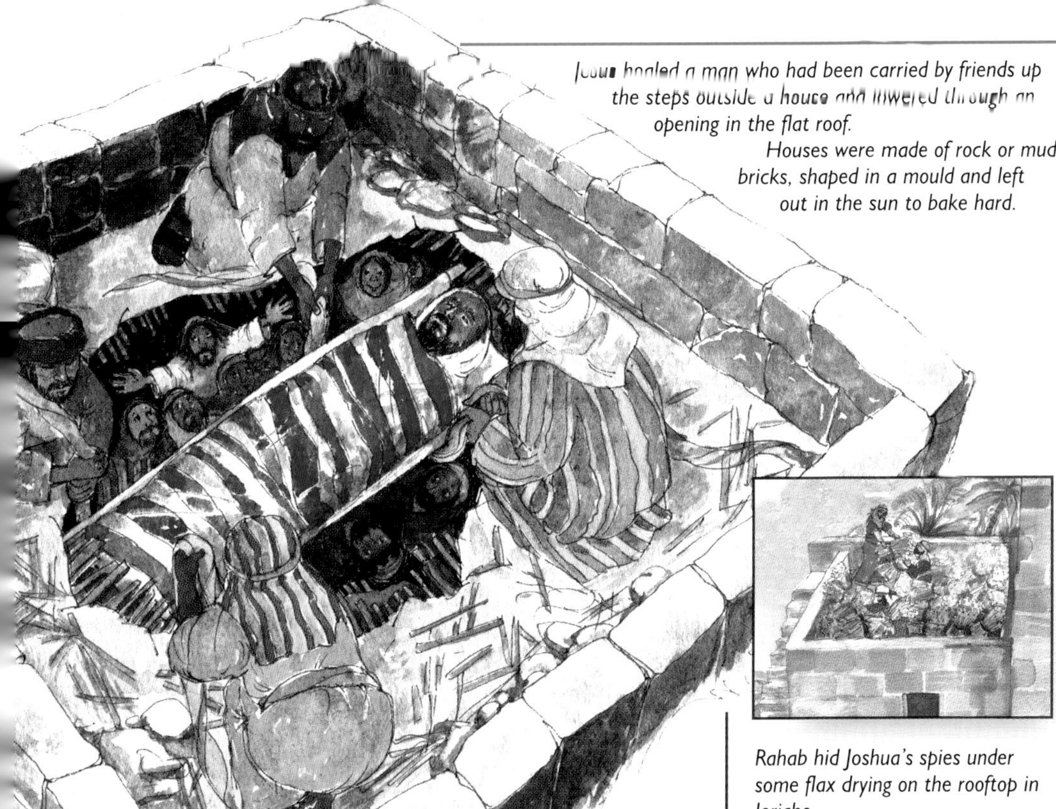

Jesus healed a man who had been carried by friends up the steps outside a house and lowered through an opening in the flat roof.

Houses were made of rock or mud bricks, shaped in a mould and left out in the sun to bake hard.

Rahab hid Joshua's spies under some flax drying on the rooftop in Jericho.

- **Windows** The small windows had no glass, but wooden shutters kept out unwanted visitors at night.
- **Floors** These were usually made of trodden-down earth.
- **Animal shelter** In country areas, people sometimes brought their animals indoors on cold nights. Such houses may have had a raised area where the family slept and ate, leaving the lower area for the animals.
- **Community** Several small houses might be built around a yard where everyone did their cooking and washing. Different members of the same family lived in the little rooms. Water had to be fetched from the local well.

Rich people's houses

- **Courtyard** Bigger houses were often built around a courtyard. Some houses had an upstairs, which was reached by outside steps from the courtyard. The courtyard was used for cooking and washing. The animals could be kept here, too.
- **Water** People who could afford big houses chose to build them close to a water supply, and often had their own well.
- **Decoration** Sometimes the walls were plastered and decorated with pictures or mosaics, or they were lined with cedar wood. The floor might be covered with mud plaster.

Inside

- **Light** Most houses were very dark. Most of the light came through the door, which was kept open in the daytime. Oil lamps were the only light after sunset. Most people went to bed then, and woke up with the dawn.
- **Heat** Although it was usually hot in the day, it was colder at night and in winter. An open fire was used for heating and cooking inside small houses, making them smoky. Rich Roman villas in New Testament times had a central heating system called a "hypocaust" in which warm air was channelled through flues in the wall.
- **Bathing** Rich houses might have had bathrooms, but poor people washed in the open, or not at all. King David was able to see Bathsheba take a bath from his rooftop.
- **Furniture** The furniture in poor houses was basic. People probably slept on the floor on a mattress stuffed with hair or straw, or on a simple wooden bed. Tables were low, with people sitting on cushions on the floor. The prophet Amos records that some rich people's furniture was decorated with very expensive ivory.
- **Food storage** Grain, oil and water was stored in large earthenware jars. The biggest ones could be almost 3 feet high.

At night, the house was lit by oil-lamps placed in an alcove in the house. The wick was made of flax, and olive oil was used.

Look it up

- *The spies who hid on the rooftop* Joshua 2:2–9
- *Bathsheba takes a bath* 2 Samuel 11:2
- *Elisha stays in Shunem* 2 Kings 4:8–10
- *The parable of the two house builders* Matthew 7:24–27
- *The men who broke through the roof* Mark 2:1–5
- *Peter's rooftop vision* Acts 10:9–20
- *The man who fell out of the window* Acts 20:7–12

Connections

1) Find on page 6 how women carried water home from the well.

2) Turn to page 12 to find what sort of food was cooked for a typical main meal.

3) Find out on page 18 which early Christians were tentmakers by trade.

4) Look at page 18 to see which fruits were carved on the walls of fine buildings.

5) Discover on page 25 what Jews make at the Feast of Tabernacles to remember the time they lived in tents.

Towns and Cities

When the Israelites settled in Canaan, they began to live in houses. Villages were just a cluster of houses, but towns and cities had walls round them – essential defence from enemy forces. If an area was attacked, villagers would shelter in the town or city. In Old Testament times most cities in Israel had only a few thousand people. Cities such as Nineveh and Babylon were considerably bigger.

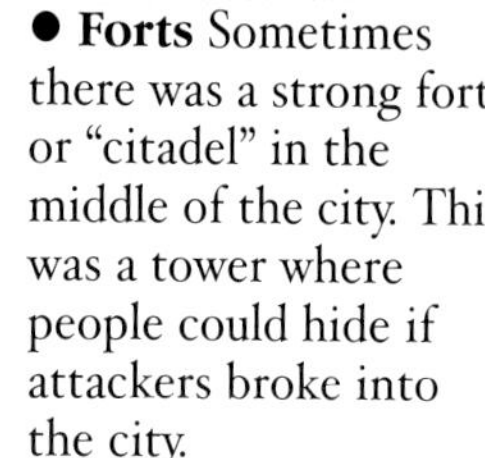

Built for defence

- **Walls** Many city walls were 15 feet thick. Semi-circular or rectangular towers were built at intervals, making the walls stronger.
- **Double walls** Two walls over 3 feet thick with a ditch about 9 feet wide in between were called "casemate" walls. Sometimes they were joined by cross walls. Houses, such as Rahab's, were built into the gap.
- **Gateways** Thick wooden doors, sometimes covered with metal to protect against fire, were good at keeping enemies out. Gateways were wide enough for carts to get through. They were locked by sliding heavy wooden beams across the two doors from the inside. 
- **Forts** Sometimes there was a strong fort or "citadel" in the middle of the city. This was a tower where people could hide if attackers broke into the city.

Water for life

- **Wells** Settlements were always built near a water supply. Village women went to the well every morning to fetch water. They carried it home in pots on their heads, or in sewn-up animal skins slung over the backs of donkeys.
- **Cisterns** Rainwater was often collected in big tanks called "cisterns", dug into the rock. Both Joseph and Jeremiah, at different times, were flung into dry cisterns.
- **Tunnels** Cities had to have a good water supply which attackers could not cut off. In Jerusalem, King Hezekiah built a long tunnel from a stream outside the city to carry water into the Pool of Siloam.
- **Aqueducts** By New Testament times, the Romans had built huge "aqueducts" which carried water across the country. There was one near Caesarea, the city rebuilt by Herod the Great

HEROD THE GREAT, BUILDER

Herod the Great built many large buildings and cities including Caesarea. It had a large man-made harbour for trading ships. It also had an amphitheatre, a smaller theatre for plays, a great temple and many public buildings.

He also built a huge fortress on a hill in the southern desert, at Masada. It had reservoirs and aqueducts for water, hot and cold bathhouses, two palaces, a synagogue for worship, a barracks for soldiers, houses and storerooms.

Jericho was a well-fortified city until Joshua attacked it and the walls fell down. It was not far from the River Jordan, so was an important fortress to defend Canaan against attackers from the east.

in the first century CE. The aqueduct was almost 6 miles long and brought water to the city from Mount Carmel.

Jesus was born in the small town of Bethlehem. Later he often visited an even smaller place called Bethany, where his friends Lazarus, Mary and Martha lived.

- **Drains and sewers** Before the Romans came, getting rid of waste was very primitive. A few places in Canaan (such as Beersheba) had drainage channels which took waste water and sewage out of the city. Water was often thrown into pits outside the city or village. The "Dung Gate" in Jerusalem led to the Valley of Hinnom, the city rubbish tip, which was always smouldering. Jesus used it as a picture of hell.

Street life

- **Town planning** Most towns and cities in Bible lands grew in a random fashion. Other civilisations planned their cities: by the sixth century BCE some Persian towns and cities were built like a grid. Some Greek and Roman cities followed this pattern.

- **Paving** The streets were usually narrow, like alleyways, and were paved with stones or made of trodden-down mud.
- **Markets** Most towns and cities had a market place (in Greek cities, the agora) where people bought and sold things. There were different "quarters" where particular tradespeople worked or sold their goods. In the Bible we read about Jerusalem's gates: the Fish Gate, the Sheep Gate and the "Tower of the Ovens" which was probably the bread-making quarter.

Public buildings

- **Village life** In villages people shared a grain store, a threshing area for cutting the corn from straw, and a wine press, where people squelched the grapes with their feet.
- **Store cities** The Israelite slaves in Egypt were forced to build storehouses. King Solomon built big stores in some of his cities, including Megiddo, and King Ahab built huge storehouses in Hazor.
- **Ancient buildings** Nineveh in Babylon had one of the biggest libraries of the ancient world. Babylon, where Jews such as Daniel were taken to live by King Nebuchadnezzar, had massive palaces and government buildings.

- **The Temple** King Solomon built a number of public buildings in Jerusalem, including the Temple, and his own palace. These were later destroyed by the Babylonians. The Temple was rebuilt first by Zerubbabel, and then by Herod the Great.
- **Roman style** The Romans built cities with stadiums (or amphitheatres), baths, apartment blocks and villas for rich people.

Look it up

- *The walls of Jericho Joshua 6:1–20*
- *Gideon in the wine press Judges 6:11*
- *King David invades using a water tunnel 2 Samuel 5:6–8*
- *Jerusalem's gates and quarters Nehemiah 3:1–14*
- *Paul in Damascus Acts 9:11*

Connections

1) Fish was sold at the Fish Gate in Jerusalem; find out how fish was preserved on page 12.

2) Find on page 16 what kind of simple games children played outdoors.

3) Discover on page 17 who came to sell their wares at the city gate.

4) Look at page 20 to see what kind of roads the Romans built across their empire.

5) See what enemies used to batter down the gates and destroy the walls on page 27.

The apostle Paul spent over two years in Ephesus in modern Turkey. It had a big market, a huge theatre holding 24,000 people, and the great temple of Diana.

Clothes

In Bible lands it was often very sunny, so clothes were needed to protect the skin. No clothes have survived from the time, so our information comes from wall paintings and sculptures. Most of these come from Israel's enemies, as the Israelites were forbidden to make pictures of people. The traditional clothing of people living in the same countries today has not changed very much.

Basic clothes

- **Tunic** Both men and women wore a simple, loose tunic, a length of cloth with a hole in the middle for the head. Men's tunics were knee-length; women's were ankle-length.
- **Belt** Made of cloth or leather, the belt could hold tools or money. When working, men could tuck their tunic in their belt.
- **Underwear** Men wore a simple loin-cloth. Fishermen, such as Peter, Andrew, James and John, would have taken off their tunics for hot and heavy work.
- **Cloak** A warm woollen cloak was essential on cold days, and was also used as a blanket at night. Ruth slept at Boaz's feet under his cloak to show she wanted to be his wife.

Shoes

- **Sandals** Poor people wore no shoes. Others wore simple sandals made of leather, tied on with a thong or strap.

Clothes were washed in fast flowing water or by pounding out dirt on flat stones while the clothes were wet. Olive oil was used to make soap.

People had to walk everywhere in open sandals, so it was the custom to wash guests' dusty feet when they arrived at your house. Mary did this for Jesus with expensive perfume, wiping his feet with her hair.

HEAD COVERINGS

It was important to protect your head from the intense sun. A simple piece of cloth was used which covered the head and the neck, kept in place by a band of cloth. Men sometimes wore a sort of turban. Women always wore a head covering in public, as a symbol of modesty.

Samson's braids were woven into a piece of cloth by Delilah on a horizontal loom. The introduction of the upright loom meant that wider material could be made.

Jacob gave Joseph a special long-sleeved coat, showing that he loved him more than all his other children.

Rich man *Average man* *Working man* *Rich woman* *Widow* *Working woman*

Making clothes

● **Wool** Each spring the sheep were shorn. The wool was washed several times to get rid of the grease before being spun into creamy white, dark or speckled thread. The cloth sometimes had a simple pattern or stripes woven into it. Poor people's clothes and thick outer cloaks were usually made of wool. It could be itchy.

Most people made their own clothes at home, weaving on a simple loom.

● **Linen** Richer people wore soft clothes made of linen. The stems of the flax plant were cut, dried, washed and dried again before the fibres were spun into off-white thread.

● **Dyes** The main dyes were red, blue and purple, and came from plants or shellfish. Dyeing was done in big stone basins. Lydia, one of Paul's followers, was a trader in purple cloth.

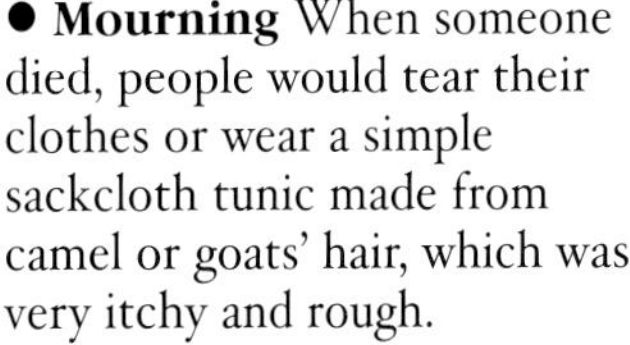

Special clothes

● **Party clothes** Most people had only one set of basic clothes. Rich people collected clothes which might be very colorful, and embroidered with patterns, or have colored fringes. Rich women wore colored scarves and shawls.

● **Weddings** Everyone was expected to dress up and a rich family might even provide wedding garments for the poorer guests. The bride would wear a veil over her face, have her hair braided with precious stones, and wear a long wedding dress in bright colors.

The different sections of clothes were sewn together by hand, although some were woven whole and had no seam.

● **Mourning** When someone died, people would tear their clothes or wear a simple sackcloth tunic made from camel or goats' hair, which was very itchy and rough.

● **Cosmetics and perfumes** Israelite women probably used perfumes made from spices mixed with olive oil or sap from trees. Women in Egypt and Rome used lipstick, eye shadow, nail varnish and face powder too.

● **Jewelery** Rich women may have worn earrings, nose-rings and necklaces, as well as bracelets on their wrists and ankles and ornate tiaras or headbands.

People from rich families dressed in more elaborate clothes, often made of purple cloth. Those with little money could not afford anything so fine.

Look it up

- *Jacob marries Leah Genesis 29:15–30*
- *Joseph's special coat Genesis 37:3–4*
- *Samson's gift of party clothes and tunics Judges 14:10–20*
- *Samuel's new robe 1 Samuel 2:18–21*
- *Isaiah's warning to rich women Isaiah 3:13–24*
- *John the Baptist's camels' hair tunic Matthew 3:4*
- *The woman who washed Jesus' feet John 12:1–7*
- *Dorcas the clothes-maker Acts 9:36–43*

Connections

1) Discover on page 10 what goats' hair and skins were often used for.

2) Find out what clothes babies wore on page 14.

3) Look at page 18 to see what animal skins were soaked in when preparing leather for sandals.

4) Discover on page 19 which shellfish was used to make purple dye.

5) See what soldiers wore when they went into battle on page 26.

PRESSING THE GRAPES

First, the grapes were put in a wine press, usually a hollow in the rocky ground, with a stone wall round it. Then people squeezed out the juice by treading on them, singing and shouting as they did so. The juice ran out through holes at the bottom of the press, where it was collected in a vat and then poured into jars, where it fermented.

STORING GRAIN

Grain (wheat or barley) was stored in big containers hollowed out from the rocky ground or in special barns. It was also kept in smaller quantities in earthenware jars at home. Joseph organized the Egyptians to store plenty of grain so they had food for years when the harvests failed.

Connections

1) Turn to page 12 to see where bread was baked.

2) Which special food was eaten at the Passover festival? Turn to page 12 to find out.

3) Look at page 20 to see which animals were called "pack animals".

4) Discover on page 22 which other dangerous wild animals prowled around the countryside.

5) Look at page 23 to see what sort of herbs and spices were grown for flavoring food and wine.

6) Find out on page 25 which religious festival was a time of thanksgiving for the harvest.

Farming and Fishing

The Bible is set in a farming world. Most people lived in the country, grew their own food, and kept animals. Even people who lived in towns often had land nearby. Farmers needed good weather at the right time of year. They depended on the food they could grow. That is why famines or food shortages are often mentioned in the Bible. Fishing was a big industry round Lake Galilee.

Animals

- **Sheep** In Old Testament times, a man's wealth was measured by the number of sheep or goats he had. Job owned 7,000 sheep and was thought to be a very wealthy man. Sheep were kept for milk, cheese and yogurt, as well as for meat and wool. People sometimes wore a sheep's fleece to keep warm. Horns from sheep were also used to store olive oil.
- **Goats** Like sheep, they were also kept for milk and meat. Their hair and skins were used for making tents and wineskins.
- **Cattle** Oxen were working animals rather than food animals. They pulled the plow or other heavy loads.
- **Donkeys and camels** Some people owned a donkey to help carry heavy loads. Camels were useful for journeys across hot, dry lands.
- **Predators** Looking after the animals could be dangerous work: lions and bears might attack sheep or young animals. There were always vultures and wild dogs looking for food. David used a sling to hurl stones at the wild animals; he once killed a bear and a lion.

Shepherds took their sheep and goats to find fresh grass. Each sheep had a name and knew the special call of its shepherd. Jesus called himself "the Good Shepherd".

Seed to harvest

- **Get ready** The farmer used a wooden plow pulled by a pair of oxen to break up the soil.
- **Sow the seed** The wheat or barley seed was scattered by hand, and was covered over by the oxen dragging tree branches over the field, or by getting animals to trample it in.
- **Harvest** When it had grown ripe, the grain was cut using a scythe. The stalks of corn were gathered into sheaves.

The farmer used a wooden plow pulled by a pair of oxen to break up the soil.

Poor people like Ruth were allowed by law to "glean" after the harvest. This meant they could take any grain left over at the edges of the fields.

- **Threshing** The next stage was to cut the ears of corn off the stalks. The stalks were spread on a hard floor (the threshing floor) and oxen pulled a special sledge, a wooden frame studded with metal or bone, over it. Gideon threshed wheat secretly in a wine press to avoid being seen by the Midianites.
- **Winnowing** The loose grain was taken outside and tossed into the air. The wind blew the straw away and the heavy grain fell to the ground in a pile. The

grain was shoveled up and put in containers, ready to be ground into flour to make bread. The straw was kept as bedding for people and animals.

Jesus' first disciples, Simon Peter, Andrew, James and John, made their living as fishermen on Lake Galilee.

Crops

- **Grapes** Vines took a long time to grow and needed careful attention. Grapes were grown to make wine and to eat in season, and some were dried to make raisins. When Moses sent spies into Canaan, they brought home huge bunches of grapes showing how fertile the land was.

- **Figs** These could be eaten fresh or dried. Abigail collected 200 cakes of dried figs to offer to David when he was in the wilderness of Paran.
- **Other cultivated plants** Beans and lentils, leeks, onions, garlic, pomegranates and dates, salad leaves, herbs and spices were grown for food.
- **Flax** This was grown to provide linen thread for weaving, and also wicks for oil-lamps. Flax was grown by the Egyptians from ancient times.
- **Olives** were eaten with bread, or pressed to make olive oil. Olive oil was used for cooking, lighting, and as a medicine. Solomon gave King Hiram of Tyre a gift of 400,000 litres of pure olive oil every year.

Fishing

- **Where?** The main fishing industry was on Lake Galilee, a large freshwater inland lake. Violent storms could blow up and swamp small fishing boats. Several of Jesus' disciples were fishermen.
- **When?** Fishing was done mainly in the evening or early morning when the fish tended to be nearer the surface. Sometimes a person standing on the shore could see the shadow of a shoal of fish and tell the fishermen where to cast their nets.
- **How?** Fishermen worked from boats, but they also waded into the water and threw large nets out to catch smaller fish near the shore. They did not use fishing lines. It was hard work.
- **What?** There were said to be twenty-four different types of fish in Lake Galilee. It was a big industry: the fish that were not eaten fresh were preserved by salting or drying. Many fish were exported from Galilee.

Olives were crushed in a special press to make olive oil.

Look it up

- *Joseph's plan to store grain in Egypt Genesis 41:29–36*
- *Ruth "gleaned" left-over grain in the fields Ruth 2*
- *David the shepherd boy killed a bear and a lion 1 Samuel 17:34–37*
- *Abigail collected cakes of dried figs 1 Samuel 25:18*
- *Solomon gave a gift of olive oil to King Hiram 1 Kings 5:11*
- *Jesus' story about a man sowing seed Matthew 13:1–23*
- *Jesus and the fishermen Luke 5:1–11*
- *Jesus the good shepherd John 10:1–16*
- *Jesus the true vine John 15:1–10*

THE WATCHTOWER

There was often a stone watchtower overlooking the land so that someone could guard the crops against thieves.

SWEETENERS

There was no sugar in Bible times. People used honey which was gathered from bee hives in the wild. Syrup was made by boiling grape juice or the pods and beans from the locust bean (carob) tree.

PRESERVING

There were two ways of doing this: salting and drying. Fruit was often laid out to dry in the sun on the roof of the house. Dried cakes of figs or raisins were very popular. Around Lake Galilee, some fish were covered in salt and laid out in the sun to dry.

FOOD LAWS

God's people had some rules about which animals they should not eat. These laws protected them against infection in a hot country where food goes bad very quickly. They could eat cattle, sheep or goats, but not pigs, shellfish, rabbits, camels or certain birds.

PASSOVER MEAL

This special meal was eaten once a year, to remind God's people of how God rescued them from slavery in Egypt. Unleavened bread (bread made without yeast) was eaten as a sign of being ready to leave. Roast lamb and bitter herbs (to remind them of their suffering) and a special sauce were eaten at the Passover Festival, with wine to drink. Jesus met with his disciples for the Passover meal – the Last Supper – shortly before his death.

Food and Drink

Eating together was at the heart of family and community life. No celebration or festival was complete without a feast! Most people in villages grew their own grain, fruit and vegetables and kept their own animals.

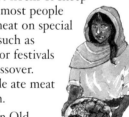

Quail flew low over the ground, so they were easy to catch and eat.

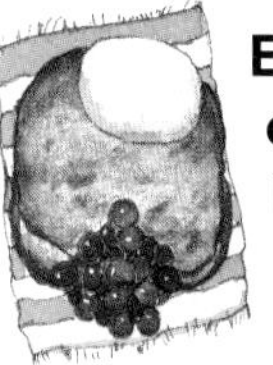

Everyday food

- **Bread** "To eat bread" meant to have a meal together. Bread, made from barley or wheat, was the most important food. It was eaten at every meal.
- **Olives** Used as oil, or pickled, olives were an important part of the meal.
- **Vegetables** The family ate whatever fresh vegetables were in season – onions, leeks, cucumbers, lentils and beans. Esau was willing to sell his birthright for a bowl of Jacob's tasty stew of lentils and beans.
- **Fruit** Seasonal fruit included pomegranates, figs, dates, mulberries and grapes. Figs, dates and raisins were also dried and pressed into cakes.
- **Cheese or yogurt** This was made from the milk of sheep or goats.
- **Fish** Near Lake Galilee, people ate fresh or dried fish.
- **Herbs and spices** These were used to flavor the food: dill, cumin, mint, coriander.

Drink

- **Wine** As water was often not safe to drink, wine was the everyday drink for adults.
- **Milk** Most households had a pet sheep or goat which was milked every day.

Special food

- **Meat** Although many people kept flocks of sheep and goats, most people only had meat on special occasions such as weddings, or festivals like the Passover. Rich people ate meat more often.
- **Game** In Old Testament times, hunters like Esau caught deer or gazelle.

Jesus often shared meals with people as he taught them about God's kingdom. When he went to the house of a tax-collector, the religious authorities were shocked.

Miraculous food

- **Manna and quail** After the Israelites escaped from Egypt, they lived in the Sinai desert for forty years. God provided water out of a rock; manna – a white, honey-flavored substance – on the ground each morning; and also flocks of quail, a small game bird, to cook and eat.

A loaf of bread

- **Grinding corn** Most people grew barley, but richer people could afford wheat. The women would grind the grain into flour using a hand-mill or a pestle and a mortar.
- **Making dough** The flour was made into dough by adding salt and water, and a little bit of leaven (yeast) kept from the mix of the day before. It was left in the sun to rise.
- **Baking bread** The flat pieces of dough were stuck on the walls of a hot clay oven. Fresh bread was made every day.

Mealtimes

- **Breakfast** This was a simple meal of bread, with olives, cheese or fruit.
- **Main meal** After the day's work was finished, the ordinary family gathered together to eat a vegetable or lentil stew flavored with herbs and spices. This was eaten from one pot, using a piece of bread to scoop out the stew.

Feasts

● **Weddings** The whole community was invited to a wedding and it was a great opportunity for singing and dancing, eating and drinking.

● **Thanksgivings** A number of Jesus' parables (stories) were about feasts. He told one about a son who ran away. When the boy came home, his father held a great feast and killed the prize calf for the feast. Families also celebrated the birth of a new baby.

● **Religious festivals** There were specific times in the year when people thanked God and celebrated with special meals.

● **Visitors** Throughout Bible times, it was the custom to welcome strangers who were passing through your village and to offer them food and drink and somewhere to stay. This was also the opportunity for a special meal!

Look it up

- *Abraham offers food and shelter to strangers Genesis 18:1–8*
- *Esau sells his "birthright" to Jacob for some lentil stew Genesis 25:27–34*
- *The first Passover meal Exodus 12:1-28*
- *Manna and quail in the desert Exodus 16:1–18*
- *Jesus eats at Simon the Pharisee's house Luke 7:36–50*
- *Jesus' story about the runaway son Luke 15:11–24*
- *Jesus at a wedding feast John 2:1–11*
- *Jesus feeds more than 5000 people John 6:1–13*
- *The Last Supper Matthew 26:17–30*
- *Peter has a vision of "unclean" food Acts 10:10–16*

Connections

1) Find out on page 10 which kind of seed farmers planted in the fields.

2) Which animals did farmers rear for food? Find out on page 10.

3) Discover on page 17 for which three festivals people had to go to Jerusalem.

4) Search page 23 to see which foods came from trees.

5) Who brought spices to Bible lands? See page 23.

Family

BABY CARE

To keep a baby's skin soft and clean, myrtle leaves were ground to a soft powder and rubbed on the skin. Olive oil was often used to clean and moisturize the skin.

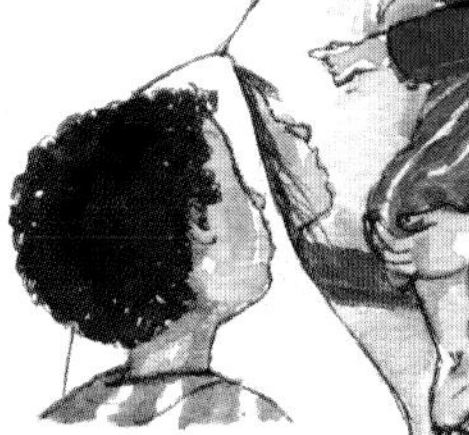

Babies and children were welcomed and loved by the community. Mothers brought children to Jesus to be blessed, even though his disciples discouraged it.

In Bible times, families included parents and children, aunts and uncles, grandparents, cousins and even servants. In the Old and New Testaments, each Jewish family belonged to a tribe, and the tribes made up the nation of God's people.

Like all new-born babies, Jesus was wrapped in swaddling clothes. It was not unusual for a baby to have a manger for its cot.

Babies and children

- **Babies** New-born babies were rubbed with salt and wrapped up in "swaddling clothes" – like wide bandages. People believed that this would help a child's legs and arms to grow straight.
- **Thanksgiving** On the eighth day, parents took their baby to the Temple and offered a sacrifice to God. Jesus was taken to the Temple in Jerusalem. Boys were circumcized as a sign that they belonged to the people of God.

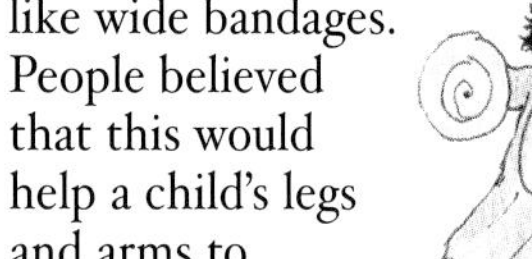

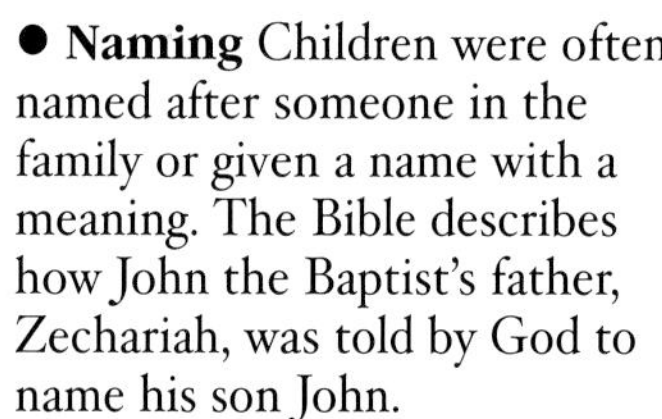

A WEDDING CELEBRATION

After the betrothal came the wedding. The groom went to the bride's house, usually in the evening, then took her back to his house, accompanied by everyone in the village in a joyful procession. The party and the celebrations sometimes lasted as long as one week.

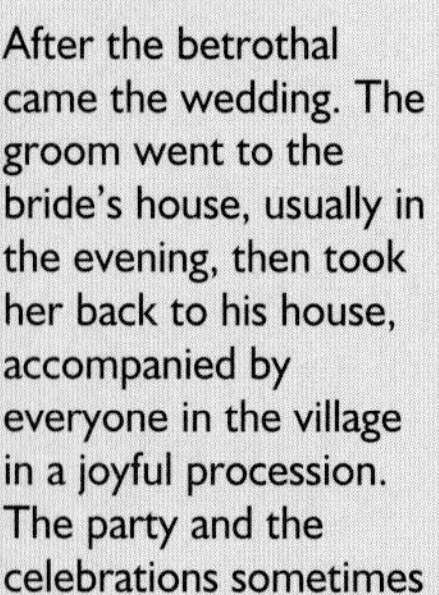

When Mary and Joseph brought their offering of two young pigeons to the Temple, Simeon knew that Jesus was God's chosen one, the Messiah.

- **Naming** Children were often named after someone in the family or given a name with a meaning. The Bible describes how John the Baptist's father, Zechariah, was told by God to name his son John.
- **Growing up** Children were responsible for some everyday tasks in the home. At the age of about thirteen, a child became "grown up". In New Testament times (and still today) a boy had his *bar mitzvah*, or coming-of-age ceremony. He became "a son of the law" and was treated as an adult.

Family life

- **Men** Each family was like a little community, with the father in charge. Home was the place where laws had to be kept because there was no local or national government.

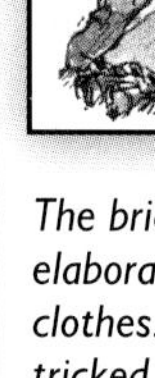

The bride wore elaborate wedding clothes. Jacob was tricked into marrying Leah instead of Rachel because she was wearing a veil.

Women Women were not
lowed to teach in synagogues.
heir work was home-based,
aring for the family. Jesus was
evolutionary in the way he had
omen disciples and friends
ich as Mary and Martha.

Faith Over meals and at
eligious festivals, families
hared the stories of their faith.
or the Jews, wisdom was more
nportant than knowledge.
Wisdom was living God's
way.

● **Land** Each family had a piece of land. When the father died, the eldest son became head of the family. This meant the family always had somewhere to live and work. Jesus told the parable of the Prodigal Son, where the younger son of a family wanted his inheritance before his father's death.

Wedding celebrations went on for a whole week. The whole community attended the wedding feast. At a wedding feast in Cana, Jesus turned water into wine.

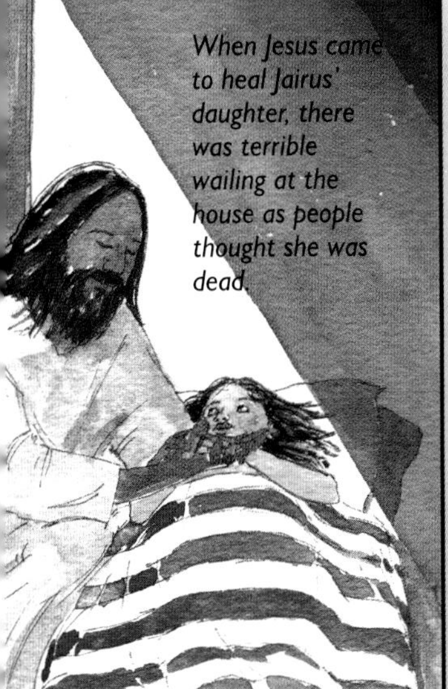

When Jesus came to heal Jairus' daughter, there was terrible wailing at the house as people thought she was dead.

Marriage and children

● **Marriage** In Old Testament times men were allowed more than one wife, but by New Testament times, Jews and Christians usually only had one partner. Families were generally big.

● **Weddings** There was always a betrothal or engagement first, arranged by the couple's parents. This was a legal contract: the man's father paid the bride's father some money and the bride's father gave his daughter or her new husband a present or dowry.

● **Divorce** A man could divorce his wife, but not the other way round. It was meant to be extremely rare – usually only if the woman had gone away with another man. But by the time of Jesus, a man could divorce his wife if she burned his meal! That was not how the law was intended to be used, Jesus taught.

Funerals

● **Mourning** Funerals were community events. The older women in a village would lead the procession to the burial place, wailing and tearing their clothes.

● **Grave clothes** Bodies were wrapped in tight bandages, and spices were put between the layers.

● **Burial** The body was placed in a cave, which would then be sealed. These burial caves usually belonged to families. Bodies were laid on a ledge in the cave. Later, when the bones were left, they were taken and put into a small stone box called an ossuary. Burial places were "unclean" to strict Jews and tombs were painted white so people could avoid them.

● **Widows and orphans** Widows and disabled people had to rely on their families to feed and house them. When Ruth's first husband died, Ruth stayed with her mother-in-law, Naomi, and married Naomi's relative Boaz who then looked after them both.

On the day of the resurrection, Mary Magdalene took herbs and spices to Jesus' tomb to anoint his body. When she got there, the massive stone across the entrance had been rolled back. Jesus, who had risen from the dead, met her in front of the tomb.

Look it up

- *The meaning of the name "Jesus" Matthew 1:18–21*
- *Jesus's story about a wedding feast Matthew 22:1–14*
- *A night-time bridal procession Matthew 25:1–13*
- *Jesus brings Jairus' daughter back to life Mark 5:21–42*
- *The naming of John the Baptist Luke 1:57–66*
- *Lazarus is buried John 11:17–44*

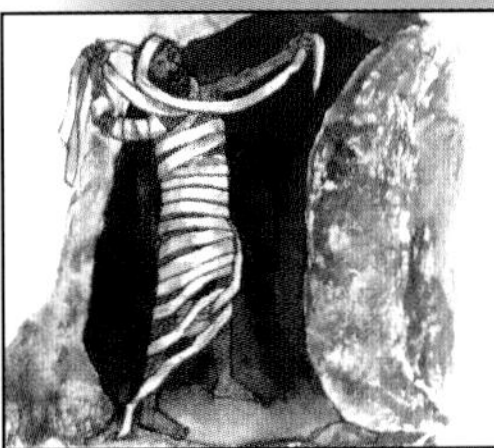

When Jesus raised Lazarus to life, he came out of the tomb still wearing his grave clothes.

Connections

1) Where did women weave thread to make clothes? Find out on page 9.

2) Discover what people offered to visitors on page 13.

3) Mealtimes were the center of family life; see page 16 to discover where they cooked food.

4) Look at page 17 to see what boys learned at synagogue school.

5) Find out on page 18 who had workshops next to their homes.

CHILDREN'S GAMES

Children in a village would play outdoor games together such as hide-and-seek, hopscotch, blind man's buff and tug-of-war. Archaeologists have found remains of other children's toys – hoops, rattles, spinning tops and board games like chess or draughts. Jesus himself talked about some of the "pretend" games children played in his day – weddings and funerals were obviously popular!

MUSIC AND STORYTELLING

Musical instruments were used in the Temple and also to entertain people for special occasions such as weddings and celebrations. There would be singing and dancing, pipes, small harps and tambourines. Telling stories was also good entertainment – many people came to hear the stories Jesus told.

GOD'S LAWS FOR LIFE

Every child learned this: "Love God with all your heart, with all your soul and with all your strength."

Fathers were told: "Teach God's commands to your children. Repeat them when you are at home and when you are away from home, when you are resting and when you are working. Write them on the doors of your house and on your gates."

Daily Life

In Bible times, everything centred on the home. Here children were educated, trades and the family's faith were passed on from parent to child.

Beds consisted of a mat on the floor which could be rolled up.

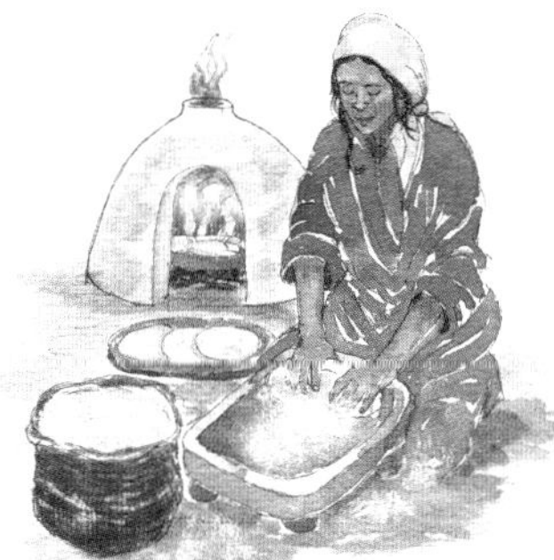

Baking bread.

Women had to fetch water from the well every day. It was also a meeting place. In the Old Testament, Abraham's servant, Eliezer, met a suitable wife for Isaac at the village well.

The working day

- **Dawn** The family woke up as soon as it was daylight. Everyone had work to do. A simple meal was eaten in the morning.
- **Women's work** Women fetched water from the well, prepared food and made clothes. Cooking was done over an open fire or in a small oven. Most meat and vegetables were stewed. For special occasions, meat was roasted on a spit (a wooden frame) over an open fire. Most women would spin and weave wool to make cloth at home.
- **Children's work** Children helped their parents with their work – the boys helped their fathers, and the girls helped their mothers.
- **Men's work** Many men were simply involved in food production. By New Testament times, craftsmen worked from home in different trades.
- **Dusk** At the end of the day, everyone met together to eat, and went to sleep with the house lit by a small oil-lamp.

Education

- **Home school** Home was the first and most important place where children were educated. Girls learned how to run the house, boys learned a trade and children were taught the Jewish scriptures and God's laws. The Ten Commandments formed the basis of daily life for everyone.
- **Synagogue school** These schools, for boys only, probably began in the period between the Old and the New Testaments (from about 400 BCE to the time of Jesus) and

vere held in the synagogue (the ewish place of worship). The abbi, the local religious leader, aught reading, writing, basic umeracy and the religious law.

Greek schools Many of the irst Gentile (non-Jewish) hristians came from a Greek-peaking background where the ducation system was quite different. Boys were taught science, philosophy and sport as well as mathematics and literature.

Each year, thousands of people came on pilgrimage to Jerusalem for the Passover festival. On the way, they camped by the road in makeshift tents. When Jesus was twelve years old, his parents traveled in a group like this and did not notice he was missing for a whole day.

Special days

- **The Sabbath** Everyone kept God's law: to have a rest on the seventh day. No one worked on the Sabbath and even household chores were kept to a minimum.
- **Festivals and pilgrimages** There were three festivals a year when people had to visit Jerusalem: the Passover, the Festival of Weeks (Pentecost), and the Festival of Tabernacles (Harvest).

Markets

- **Village life** In country areas, most people worked at home or on the land nearby. Sometimes they produced all their own food, and everything they needed, but by New Testament times, there were small markets where goods could be bought or bartered.
- **Cities and towns** The city gate was always busy and bustling. Here farmers and traders from the villages came into the town or city to sell their wares. The city gate was opened in the morning and closed at night.
- **Traders** Some goods were imported or exported. Traders brought spices and incense from lands as far away as India, modern-day Turkey, Egypt or Babylon.

The market was a noisy, bustling place where goods were bought or bartered.

Look it up

- *The Israelites celebrate with singing and dancing Exodus 15:19–21*
- *The Ten Commandments Exodus 20:1–17*
- *David the shepherd boy and his harp 1 Samuel 16:14–23*
- *Women bring their children to Jesus to be blessed Matthew 19:13–15*
- *Joseph and Mary lose Jesus in Jerusalem Luke 2:41–52*
- *At the house of Mary and Martha Luke 10:38–42*
- *The Holy Spirit comes at the Festival of Pentecost Acts 2:1–12*

Connections

1) Find out on page 7 the names of the gates in Jerusalem where traders sold their produce.

2) Discover how people crushed grapes to make wine on page 7.

3) Find out who made the doors and shutters for village houses on page 18.

4) Look at page 25 to see how musical pipes and horns were made.

Work and Money

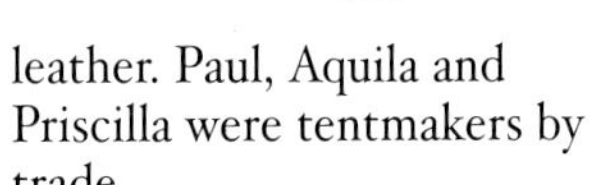

WEIGHTS AND MEASURES

In Bible times, weights and measures tended to be rather inaccurate.

• Dry measure: a homer was "a donkey load" (this would depend on the size and strength of the donkey!).

A tenth of this was an ephah, measured by a container large enough to hold a person. One tenth of an ephah was an omer, measured as a bowlful.

• Liquid measure: the standard Old Testament liquid measure was the "bath". It was about 39 pints, the size of an average storage pot.

• Lengths: based on the human body: the finger, the palm, the span of a hand, the cubit (distance from elbow to middle fingertip) and the fathom (arms extended, from one middle fingertip to the other). Longer distances, such as the distance between towns, were worked out as "a day's journey" and so on.

• Weights were usually stones, but sometimes bronze, and the value of the weight was sometimes carved onto it. The talent was a weight of silver or gold, roughly 70 lbs – although in New Testament times it seems to have been 90 lbs. It consisted of 3,000 shekels – a shekel being about 1/4 oz.

By New Testament times, many men had a trade. The workshop would be in, or next to, the family house. People used their skills to help each other and to make money to buy things they could not make themselves. In towns and cities, the market place was the center of trade and commerce.

Jesus would have learned the carpenter's trade from Joseph.

Builders and carpenters

● **Village houses** Ordinary houses were built from sun-baked mud bricks and local timber. Many people built their own homes.

● **Tools and furniture** Carpenters had a wide range of skills. They would make the roof joists, doors, door frames, shutters and furniture for village houses. They also made tools and plows for farmers, yokes for oxen and even carts. Specialist carpenters made wood carvings for fine buildings.

● **Large buildings** Jerusalem's main buildings were the Temple, official residences and the Antonia Fortress, a Roman building. These were made by skilful stonemasons who shaped the stone blocks with their tools. Solomon's Temple and fine buildings had carvings of pomegranates or vines on the stonework.

Potters

● **The potter's wheel** Plates, dishes, cups and containers were made from clay by the local potter. Jeremiah watched a potter working at his wheel, shaping the clay into pots. They were baked in a kiln – a hot oven over a fire.

● **Decoration** Pots for everyday use were plain; special pots were made of decorated colored clay, or had a pattern etched into the clay with a shaped tool or woven rope. In other countries, colored glazes were used.

Leather-workers

● **Leather goods** Tents, sandals, belts, wineskins and bottles, buckets and animal harnesses were made out of leather. Paul, Aquila and Priscilla were tentmakers by trade.

● **A tanner's life** Making leather from animal skins (from camels, goats, sheep, cattle) was messy. The hair and fat was removed from the skin, using lime or sometimes urine. Then the skins were soaked in water with leaves, oil and bark. Tanners worked on the edge of the town, where the wind carried away the smell.

Metal-workers

● **Gold and silver** Imported from nearby countries, shaped or beaten into thin sheets, gold and silver were used to decorate the Covenant Box and the Temple. Gold was also used to make fine jewelery for the high priest; he wore chains of pure gold with engraved precious stones mounted in gold settings.

● **Copper and bronze** In King Solomon's time there was a thriving copper industry on the Gulf of Aqabah – south of Israel. The ore was melted in a simple furnace, then poured into moulds. Bronze was made by adding tin to copper. Bronze was used for tools, weapons, lamps, pots and pans, and even for mirrors.

● **Iron** Iron was good for making swords, knives, plows and other tools. Iron ore was dug out of the ground, melted in a furnace and beaten into shape while hot. The best iron-

workers were the Philistines, Israel's enemies. In the time of the Judges, they had great power over the Israelites because only they could make things from iron.

Cloth-workers

● **Spinning and weaving** Most ordinary families knew how to spin and weave wool to make clothes. By late Old Testament times, there were also people who wove cloth to sell in the local market.

● **Dyes** Clothes were cream, beige, brown, grey or black, according to the sheep the wool came from. But there were also other colors: scarlet from cochineal insects; indigo and yellow from plants; and blue and purple, the most expensive dye, made from shells of the murex shellfish in the Mediterranean Sea. Only rich people could afford purple clothing. Lydia, whom Paul met in Philippi, was a trader in purple cloth.

Slaves

● **Israelite slaves** The Israelites never forgot that God had freed them from slavery in Egypt. But later King Solomon treated his own people as slaves. They did not like it and there was a rebellion when he died.

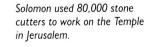

Solomon used 80,000 stone cutters to work on the Temple in Jerusalem.

● **Roman slaves** Roman slaves often had very hard lives, but some were servants of rich people and were school teachers, or civil servants, helping to administer the Roman Empire. Slaves belonged to their masters by law. Onesimus was a slave who ran away from his master, but Paul asked his master, Philemon, to forgive him.

● **Jewish law** God's Law said that slaves should be set free after seven years. In New Testament times, Paul told Christian slaves to work hard as if they were serving God and told Christian slave-owners to be fair and kind.

Look it up

- *Abraham's riches Genesis 13:2*
- *Fine jewelery for the high priest Exodus 28:9–13*
- *Miners look for precious metals underground Job 28:3–11*
- *God warns traders who use false weights and measures Micah 6:9–12*
- *Workers in the vineyard are paid a denarius Matthew 20:1–16*
- *Zacchaeus the tax collector, who climbed a sycomore-fig tree Luke 19:1–10*
- *Jesus and the money-changers in the Temple Luke 19:45–46*
- *Paul tells slaves to work hard for God Colossians 3:22 – 4:1*
- *Paul asks Philemon to forgive Onesimus Philemon 15–20*

Connections

1) Look on page 9 to find out at which time of year sheep were shorn.

2) See which animals pulled the wooden plows made by carpenters on page 10.

3) Which color was Herod's Temple in Jerusalem? See page 24.

4) Find out on page 25 on which day of the week all workers had a rest.

5) Metal-workers made bronze or iron blades for which weapons on page 26?

Trade and Travel

CAMEL CARAVANS

Camels could travel long distances and did not need water for several days. A camel "train" could be hundreds of animals long. The goods were carried in large bags carried on the camels' backs. Joseph traveled to Egypt with a camel train when his brothers sold him to the Ishmaelites. Their camels were loaded with spices.

From earliest times, traders carrying spices, gold and precious goods traveled through Bible lands, north-west from Egypt to modern-day Turkey, and north-east to Babylon. King Solomon traded by land and by sea, and by the time of Jesus, there were many trade routes in the region. Trade was also carried out locally in market places. Travel was always difficult, and often dangerous.

IMPORTED RELIGIONS

Both King Solomon and King Ahab married princesses from other nations, perhaps with a view to improving trade. These women brought with them their own pagan religions – the worship of other gods and idols. As a result, these kings, and others that followed, turned away from worshiping God and began to worship idols.

By land

- **Walking** Most people did not own a donkey, so they carried their goods to and from market, and made their local journeys on foot.
- **Pack animals** Donkeys, mules and camels carried goods, with their owners walking beside them. Carts were pulled by oxen for local journeys.
- **Horses** could cover about 25 miles in a day, but were only used by messengers or kings. Chariots pulled by horses were used by kings and leaders of the army.
- **Messengers** They walked, ran or rode from place to place, carrying messages from rulers to their assistants. In the days of the early church, Paul used messengers to take his letters to churches in many different places.

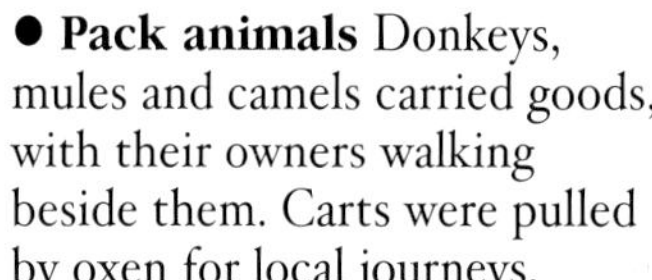

Roads

- **Tracks** To start with, travelers followed the tracks made when farmers moved their flocks from one grazing place to another. Other routes were made by merchants or invading or ruling armies as they made their way across the country.
- **Roads** First the Persians began a road-building programme, and then the

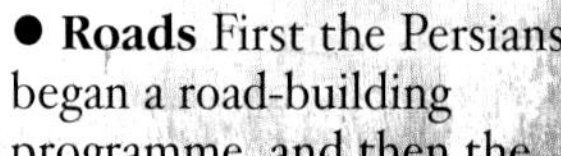

Romans built a network of paved roads across their empire. This made travel easier and quicker. Even so, Paul and his friends covered huge distances on foot across the Roman Empire, to tell people the good news of Jesus.

- **Dangers** People usually traveled in large groups for fear of being attacked and robbed. Jesus' story of the Good Samaritan describes an attack on a lonely road.
- **Overnight stops** In New Testament times, there were only a few inns and they were

Paul was shipwrecked off the coast of Malta in the autumn storms on his journey to Rome.

often unpleasant places. Travelers usually camped in their own tents, and carried all the food they needed for the journey. The Romans introduced proper staging posts where horses could be changed and food bought.

Ordinary men and women walked from place to place. Some used donkeys to carry loads. Only army commanders and the rich had horses or chariots.

By sea

● **Sailing nations** Although travel by boat was common on the huge inland Lake Galilee, the Israelites (God's people of the Old Testament) had no natural harbors on the Mediterranean coast and disliked the sea. The Phoenicians, who lived around Tyre and Sidon further north, were the best sailors. King Solomon hired Phoenician sailors and boats when he needed them.

● **Ships** The largest Roman cargo ships were about 230 feet long, powered by sails and oars. There were no instruments to help sailors find their way across the sea so most ships sailed close to the shore and put in to port every night. Sailors navigated by the stars – when they could see them.

● **Dangers** There were many storms on the Mediterranean Sea, particularly between November and March. Paul was shipwrecked off the coast of Malta in the autumn storms on his journey to Rome.

Traders

● **Local traders** Everyday farming produce (wheat, wine, grapes and figs) plus pottery and cloth were sold in the local market place.

● **Trading nations** Israel and Judah were comparatively backward countries: the great traders of Old Testament times were Babylon to the east and Tyre on the Mediterranean coast. In New Testament times, the Roman Empire had transformed trading opportunities with its excellent network of roads and sea routes. Imported items included cotton, silk, apples, glassware and slaves.

● **King Solomon's riches** Until the time of the kings, Israel was almost self-sufficient: farmers produced food for themselves and local craftsmen made everything else needed for a simple everyday existence. Even in the time of the kings, exports from Israel were agricultural: wheat, olive oil,

honey and spices. But Solomon traded these for cedar wood to build the Temple, horses and chariots, gold, silver, ivory and precious stones, as well as some more unusual imports such as monkeys and peacocks!

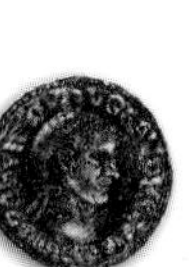

Look it up

- *Joseph travels to Egypt with a camel train*
  Genesis 37:25–28
- *Solomon hires Phoenician merchant ships*
  1 Kings 9:27–28
- *The Queen of Sheba's wealth*
  1 Kings 10:1–13
- *King Solomon imports luxury goods*
  1 Kings 10:14–29
- *Jesus tells a story about a traveler attacked by bandits*
  Luke 10:25–37
- *Paul is shipwrecked in a storm*
  Acts 27
- *Paul sends Tychicus as his messenger*
  Colossians 4:7–9

Connections

1) Discover on page 7 in which city you could have found one of the largest libraries of the ancient world.

2) See page 8 to find out a common custom for welcoming hot, dusty travelers.

3) Find out who made carts on page 18.

4) Solomon imported peacocks: which other birds on page 22 visited Israel as they migrated from Africa to Europe?

5) Find out on page 24 the names of two Canaanite gods made known to Israel by pagan queens.

The Natural World

SACRIFICES

In Old Testament times, animal sacrifices were an important part of the Jewish religion. Goats, oxen and sheep, as well as doves and pigeons, were presented to God in a special ceremony in the Temple. Mary and Joseph took this offering to Jerusalem when they presented Jesus at the Temple.

In Bible times, people were very dependent on natural resources from the land around them. Their food and building materials came primarily from the local land, lakes, hills and trees. The Bible is full of images of the colourful wildlife of the lands in and around Israel, a natural habitat for many wild animals, flowers and trees. People were very vulnerable to changes in the weather and the effect it had on their harvests.

Animals

- **Fierce wild animals** Every shepherd had to keep his sheep and goats safe from dangerous predators such as lions, leopards, bears and foxes, jackals, hyenas and wild dogs.

- **Harmless wild animals** Deer and gazelle were hunted for food. The rock hyrax was about the size of a rabbit, with small ears and no tail.
- **Animals for food** Sheep and goats were kept for meat, and milked to produce cheese and yogurt.
- **Working animals** Most people kept a donkey to help carry heavy loads or to turn a wheel stone to grind corn: donkeys were strong and cheap to feed. Sometimes people owned a mule, a cross between a horse and a donkey. Oxen were even stronger. Camels were good for journeys across hot, dry lands. Only kings and army commanders rode horses.
- **Reptiles and insects** Harmless lizards and geckos were everywhere. A plague of locusts could strip an entire crop of wheat in seconds. Moses warned the pharaoh of Egypt that there would be plagues of frogs and locusts if he did not let the Israelite slaves leave. All the crops were devastated. Lizards helped keep houses free of insects by eating them.

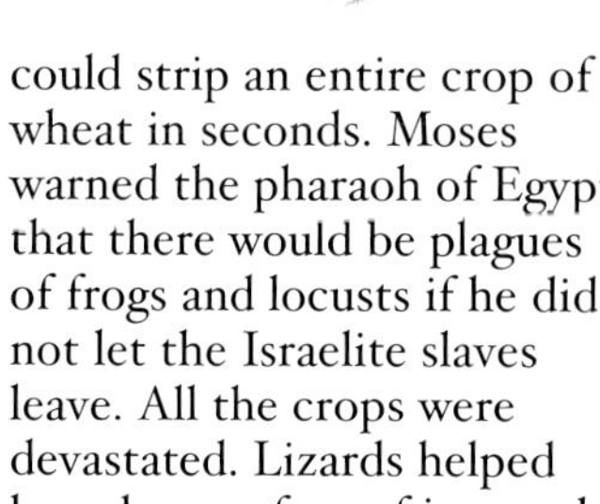

People had to beware of snakes, scorpions and flies.

Birds

- **Doves and pigeons** The wild rock-dove lived in holes and ledges in the desert, but in Bible times the turtle-dove was farmed. All doves were "clean", according to Jewish food laws, and so were eaten and also used as sacrifices. Even the poorest family could afford two doves for a sacrifice of thanksgiving at the Temple in Jerusalem.
- **Chickens** By the time of Jesus, people had begun to keep chickens for meat and for eggs.
- **Sparrow** The common house sparrow was an everyday sight. Jesus once told people that God knows everything – even when a single sparrow dies.
- **Migratory birds** Many birds pass over Israel in spring as they fly from Africa to their summer breeding grounds in Europe. In autumn they make the return journey. These include the crane, the stork, the

Connections

1) Find out which weapon was used to kill lions and bears on page 10.

2) See what olive oil was used for on page 11.

3) Discover on page 19 which tax collector climbed up into a sycomore-fig tree.

4) Find out on page 21 which unusual animals and birds King Solomon imported.

5) Look at page 24 to find which building was lined with cedar wood.

swallow and the quail. Moses and the Israelite people caught low-flying quail to eat in the desert.

- **Game birds** As well as keeping doves and pigeons to eat, people hunted birds such as the rock partridge.
- **Birds of prey** Shepherds protected their new lambs from being attacked by birds such as kites, eagles, hawks, falcons, harriers and owls. All these were "unclean", and were not eaten by humans.

Plants

- **Cereal crops** Wheat and barley were used to make loaves every day.
- **Pulses** Beans, lentils and chick peas, provided protein and were used to thicken stews and soups, as Jacob did when he cooked Esau a stew and tricked him out of his birthright.
- **Vegetables** Mallow, sorrel and artichokes, were grown so that their green leaves could be cooked and eaten. Onions, leeks and cucumbers, were either eaten raw or cooked.
- **Flowers** The hills of Galilee were covered with wild flowers including blue hyacinth, anemones, yellow chrysanthemum, white daisy and narcissus.
- **Herbs and spices** Cumin, dill, cinnamon and mint were used as flavorings for food and wine; cassia, spikenard and aloes were used as cosmetics. Merchants from Africa and Arabia exported spices, frankincense, myrrh and spikenard.
- **Flax** was an important crop used for making linen for clothes, string, nets, sails, and wicks for oil lamps.

Fish

- **Sperm whale** The Old Testament talks about the great fish and sea monsters which swam in "the Great Sea" (the Mediterranean).
- **Freshwater fish** Although Israel borders the Mediterranean Sea, Jewish people did not generally fish the sea. The large inland water, Lake Galilee, was famous for its fish, including tilapia, trout, and perch.

The tilapia, often known as St Peter's fish, is one of the most common in Lake Galilee. It was named after Peter, one of Jesus' closest friends, a fisherman.

Trees

- **Trees for food** The vine provided grapes for food and for wine. Other food came from the date palm, the fig, the mulberry, the pomegranate and the carob bean, as well as nuts from the almond and the pistachio trees. The sycomore-fig was a wild fig tree. The olive tree was also extremely important for food and oil.
- **Desert trees** The only large tree to thrive in the desert was the acacia, a spreading thorny tree, used by the Israelites for making the Covenant Box.

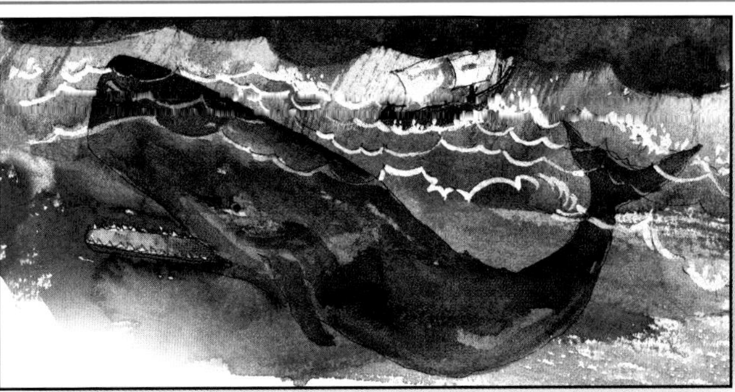

Was Jonah swallowed by a sperm whale? The Bible story says only that he was swallowed by "a big fish".

- **Hillside trees** Sacrifices were often made under terebinth trees because they offered a lot of shade, as did the oak.
- **Evergreens** Firs, pines, cedars and cypress and juniper were all used in building. Lebanon, in the north, was famous for cedars. Cypress wood was especially useful in ship-building and cedar was used in King Solomon's extravagant building projects. The Bible describes how Noah built the ark out of cypress wood.
- **Riverside trees** A number of trees grew beside streams and rivers and at oases, including willows and poplars. The tamarisk had distinctive feathery branches and tassels of pink and white flowers. The balsam poplar had a beautiful scent.

To build Solomon's Temple, cedars from Lebanon were hauled down to the sea and floated down the coast, then transported to Jerusalem.

Look it up

- *An ark of cypress wood* Genesis 6:9 –22
- *Abraham builds an altar by the trees at Mamre* Genesis 13:14–18
- *Esau hunts for meat* Genesis 27:1–4
- *God sends locusts to Egypt* Exodus 10:12–15
- *Quail for hungry Israelites in the desert* Exodus 16:13
- *Solomon sends for cedar wood* 2 Chronicles 2:1–16
- *Job's wealth measured in flocks and animals* Job 1:1–3
- *Jesus draws attention to God at work in nature* Matthew 6:25–32
- *Jesus' parents offer a sacrifice of doves in the Temple* Luke 2:22–24

Worship and Festivals

In the courtyard of the tent of meeting the people gathered to hear God's Law, to offer sacrifices, to say prayers, and to praise God in words and music.

Inside the tent, where only the priests could go, was an altar where incense was burned, a golden lampstand and a table with special loaves.

Only the high priest could enter the inner tent, the Most Holy Place, once a year. Here the Covenant Box was kept, and here God was believed to be present.

The Israelites were different from the other nations around them who worshiped many gods, for God commanded, "Worship no God but me." The Old Testament is the story of the relationship of God with his special people, starting with Abraham; and God's covenant: "You shall be my people; and I will be your God."

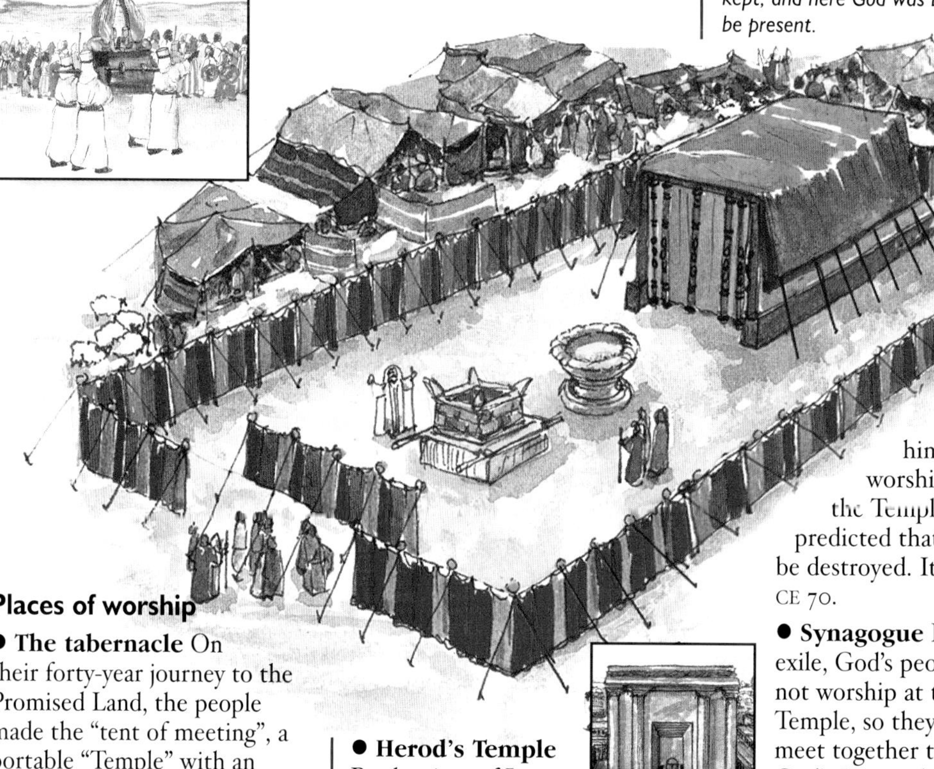

OTHER RELIGIONS

The Israelites were surrounded by nations who worshiped gods and idols: gods of weather, fertility and good luck. The Israelites showed no interest in worshiping Egyptian gods while they were in slavery, or Babylonian gods while in exile, but for the rest of the time they were constantly tempted to worship Canaanite gods, such as Baal, the storm god, or Astarte, the fertility goddess.

PROPHETS

Prophets were good and holy people, chosen by God. Isaiah foretold the coming of Jesus. The message of the prophets was frequently a reminder to turn away from idols and back to God, or to stop cheating and lying, and to treat other people fairly. The Old Testament prophets were often unpopular and had to face danger and opposition. Elijah had to run for his life after challenging the prophets of Baal to a contest which showed that God was mightier than the pagan gods.

Places of worship

- **The tabernacle** On their forty-year journey to the Promised Land, the people made the "tent of meeting", a portable "Temple" with an outer courtyard. The tent had curtains in purple, red and blue, and an animal-skin covering for a roof. The tabernacle was like a visual aid, reminding the people that God was always with them.
- **Solomon's Temple** More than 300 years later, King Solomon built a magnificent Temple where people could worship God. The stone walls were paneled with carved cedar wood, and lined with gold. The people came into the courtyard to worship God and make sacrifices. This Temple was destroyed by the Babylonians in 597 BCE, but was rebuilt under the leadership of Ezra and Zerubbabel.
- **Herod's Temple** By the time of Jesus, a new Temple made of white stone towered above all the other buildings in Jerusalem. Begun in 19 BCE, it was an impressive sight. Jesus himself worshiped at the Temple, but predicted that it would be destroyed. It was – in CE 70.
- **Synagogue** During the exile, God's people could not worship at the Temple, so they began to meet together to hear God's Law and to pray in synagogues. After the exile, the synagogue became the center of village life. The rabbi (teacher) taught all the men and boys the Jewish laws, and the Scriptures were read. Boys were educated there during the week.

The Passover Festival was a reminder of how God saved the Israelites from slavery in Egypt

● **The early church** The first followers of Jesus met in the Temple in Jerusalem to pray and worship God, but as the good news about Jesus spread from town to town and region to region, people began meeting in their houses. The word "church" does not mean a building, but a group of believers.

Temple worship

● **Priests** Descended from Aaron, the brother of Moses, priests offered sacrifices and prayers on behalf of the people. They had special clothes, and had to carry out the Temple rituals. They had to teach the people about God, and live good lives. The high priest had special responsibilities.

● **Levites** From the tribe of Levi, the Levites helped the priests. They worked as doorkeepers and musicians.

● **Sacrifices** These were a way of giving thanks to God – people had to offer their best animals, or a grain offering to God. It was also a way of receiving God's forgiveness for sins.

Abraham was prepared to sacrifice the very best thing he had – his son, Isaac – but God stopped him and Abraham offered a ram instead.

● **The Law** The word "Law" applies both to stories about God and his people (in the Old Testament) or actual laws, such as the Ten Commandments. People were taught God's Law, so that they could live in a way that pleased him.

● **Music and psalms** As a boy, David played the harp for King Saul. When he became king, David wrote many of the psalms and organized a Temple choir and orchestra. Moses' sister, Miriam, led the Israelites in dancing with tambourines and singing when God helped them cross the Red Sea.

King David himself played a kinnor, or harp. There were also many different percussion instruments, pipes (made out of reeds) and trumpets or horns (made out of animal horns).

Special days and festivals

● **The Sabbath** started on Friday evening, and went on until Saturday evening. It was a special day when no one worked, and everyone worshiped God. The first Christians decided to make Sunday their day of rest, as a reminder that Jesus rose from the dead on that day.

● **Passover** was one of the three main festivals. By the time of Jesus, most Jews went to the Temple in Jerusalem at Passover. Jesus was arrested and put on trial during the days of the Passover celebrations in Jerusalem. The Christian festival of Easter is now celebrated at the same time as the Passover.

● **Pentecost** Also known as the Festival of Weeks, this was a thanksgiving festival for the beginning of the harvest, fifty days after Passover. It was at Pentecost that God sent the Holy Spirit, as Jesus had promised.

● **Tabernacles** In autumn, people thanked God for the harvest. Shelters were made out of palm leaves and people slept outdoors, as a reminder of how God's people had slept in tents in the desert.

● **Day of Atonement** also known as Yom Kippur: at this festival, the high priest performed special ceremonies to take away the sins of the people and cleanse the Temple.

● **Other festivals** Purim: Jews remembered the time when Esther saved the Jewish people from slaughter.

Jesus turned the money-changers out of the Temple courts, telling them that they had turned a place of prayer into a place of cheating.

Solomon's Temple in Jerusalem was the center for worship in the kingdom of Judah.

Look it up

- *God's covenant with Abraham Genesis 17:1–8*
- *The Ten Commandments Exodus 20:1–17*
- *Making the tabernacle Exodus 36:2–38*
- *David brings the Covenant Box to Jerusalem 2 Samuel 6:1–5; 12–15*
- *Solomon builds the Temple 1 Kings 6*
- *Jesus is taken to the Temple as a baby Luke 2:22–40*
- *Jesus predicts the destruction of the Temple Luke 21:5,6*
- *Jesus eats a Passover meal Matthew 26:17–30*
- *The Holy Spirit comes at Pentecost Acts 2:1–42*

Connections

1) Find out on page 7 who first rebuilt the Temple after the Babylonians destroyed it.

2) Find out on page 14 at what age boys were treated as adults in the synagogue.

3) Which places were considered "unclean" by strict Jewish law? Find out on page 15.

4) See on page 18 who shaped the gold to decorate the Covenant Box.

5) Discover where the cedar trees used for Solomon's Temple walls grew on page 23.

Weapons and War

Roman centurions were a familiar sight in the time of Jesus. Cornelius, a Roman centurion who lived in Caesarea, was the first gentile (non-Jew) to believe in Jesus.

The Canaanite army was destroyed as all their chariots and soldiers were washed away in a flash flood.

The Old Testament story is about battles: first about Joshua and "winning" the land that God had given to his people; and then about defending it from the great superpowers of Assyria, Babylon and Persia. By the time of Jesus, the country was under the rule of the Romans, and thousands of Roman soldiers lived in Palestine.

A Philistine soldier carried a shield, a two-edged sword and a dagger. His head-dress was decorated with feathers and his weapons were iron – heavier, stronger and more effective than the bronze weapons carried by Israelites.

BIBLE RULES ABOUT WAR

The book of Deuteronomy in the Old Testament contains some rules about going to war:

"When you go to war and see a huge army in front of you, don't be afraid because God is with you, and he will give you victory."

"The following men are excused from fighting in a war: a man who has just built a house but has not dedicated it; a man who has planted a vineyard but has not yet harvested it; a man who is engaged to be married."
Deuteronomy 20:5–9

MAKING WEAPONS

By the time of Saul, the Philistines had removed all the blacksmiths from Israel. The Israelites were then short of swords and spears, and had to go to the Philistines to get their farming tools such as plows, axes and sickles sharpened.

Israelite soldiers

- **Fighting men** There was no army in Israel until the time of King David. Until then, leaders would call for volunteers to fight when there was a battle.
- **God's battle** God told his people that they had to trust God to lead them. When Joshua led his soldiers to conquer Jericho; when Gideon scared away thousands of Midianite soldiers; or when David killed a fully-armed Philistine champion with a single stone; they all gave the credit to God.

By David's time, the army had spearmen, archers and slingers. The archers wore armor made of overlapping plates of iron and carried bows and arrows. The slingers and spearmen carried swords and shields. The spearmen sometimes carried a javelin as well as a spear. The spear was used in hand-to-hand fighting, but javelins were thrown by all the spearmen together against an advancing army.

Weapons and armour

- **Weapons** All soldiers carried a sword, a spear or javelin, and possibly a dagger. By David's time, Israelite soldiers also carried bows and arrows. Israelite soldiers also used a sling – as when David killed Goliath.
- **Defence** Soldiers carried a shield and wore armor: a metal helmet, a breastplate, and sometimes grieves, which protected their legs.
- **Chariots** These were not always an advantage in the rocky countryside of Israel, or in marshy areas by rivers. When Moses led the Israelites across the Red Sea, the chariots of the Egyptians who followed became stuck in the mud. A raging torrent swept away 900 Canaanite chariots fighting against the Israelites led by Deborah and Barak.

Enemies of God's people

- **Egyptians** The Israelites had made Egypt their home, but eventually became slaves there. When God released them from slavery, they escaped on foot, pursued by the pharaoh's army with 600 chariots, and soldiers armed with bows and arrows.
- **Canaanites** These people were already living in Canaan. There were also other people who wanted to settle in the land – Midianites, Ammonites, Amalekites, Amorites, Gibeonites and Perrizites. All of them had bands of fighting men.

The Israelites used trumpets or shofars to call the army to battle, and to frighten their enemies. Joshua told seven priests to blow the shofar and march round the city of Jericho before Joshua's army captured it.

• **Philistines** Known as the "sea peoples", the Philistines had come from across the Mediterranean to settle in Canaan. They waged war against the Israelites over hundreds of years, and were only defeated in the days of King Saul and King David.

• **Assyrians** The Assyrian empire was huge: its army burned cities and children, and chopped off heads and hands. In 722 BCE, the northern kingdom of Samaria fell to the Assyrians, and as many as 27,000 people were taken away as prisoners of war.

• **Babylonians** The Babylonians came to power by overcoming the Assyrians; they destroyed Jerusalem in 597 BCE, and all God's people were taken to exile in Babylon.

• **Greeks and Romans** By the time of Jesus, the land had been first ruled by the Greeks and was now under Roman rule. God's people, the Jews, longed to be free.

Tactics of war

• **Surprise and confusion** In early Old Testament times, conflicts often took the form of a raid: a gang of fighting men ambushed their enemies, took away their food and animals, and destroyed their crops and houses. Success in battle often depended on creating confusion, and tricking the enemy, as at Ai, and when Gideon attacked the Midianites.

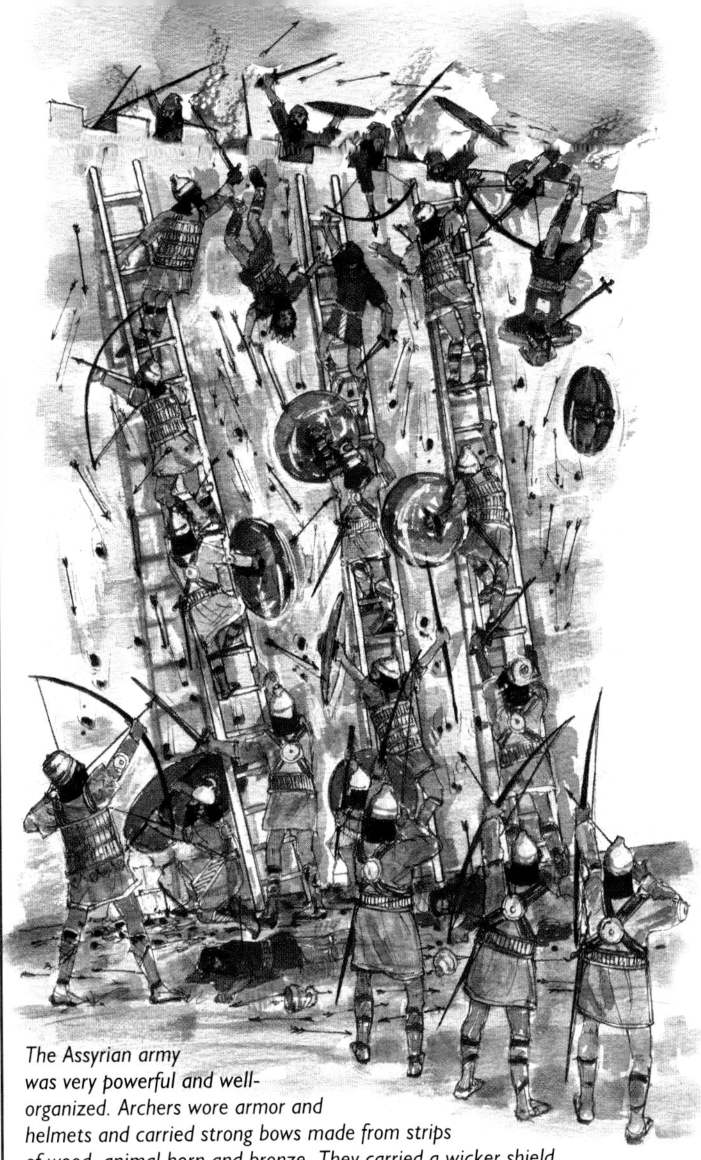

The Assyrian army was very powerful and well-organized. Archers wore armor and helmets and carried strong bows made from strips of wood, animal horn and bronze. They carried a wicker shield covered in leather to protect themselves from the arrows of the enemy.

Battering rams were used to attack a besieged city.

• **Siege** When the Babylonians besieged Jerusalem in the seventh century BCE, they surrounded the city for about eighteen months. They cut off water and food supplies, and then used siege engines and battering rams. Defenders of a city under siege would stand on the battlements and shoot at the attacking army with arrows, throw down stones and burning torches and drop boiling water on them.

• **Spoils of war** When an army raided a town or camp, they often took whatever possessions they could find as "booty". This practice was forbidden by God when the Israelites conquered Canaan. Achan disobeyed this rule and was stoned to death.

Look it up

- *Defeat of the Egyptian army* Exodus 14:1–30
- *The battle of Jericho* Joshua 6:1–25
- *Achan disobeys God* Joshua 7:1–26
- *Deborah leads Israel to victory* Judges 4:1–23
- *Gideon defeats the Midianites* Judges 7:1–21
- *David kills Goliath* 1 Samuel 17:41–51
- *The Israelites go to the Philistines to have their tools sharpened* 1 Samuel 13:19–22
- *The destruction of Jerusalem* 2 Kings 25:1–21
- *A Roman centurion's faith* Matthew 27:54

Connections

1) How many walls made a "casemate" wall? See page 6.

2) Turn to page 6 to see who built a huge fortress on a hill at Masada.

3) Find out on page 18 which metal was good for making swords.

4) Look at page 20 to see which invading nation began a road-building programme.

5) On page 22 find out which animals were used by army commanders.

Index

Numbers refer to page references.

Answers to Connections

PAGE 5

1. In pots on their heads or in sewn-up animal skins, slung over a donkey's back.
2. Vegetable or lentil stew, flavored with herbs and spices.
3. Paul, Priscilla and Aquila.
4. Pomegranates and grapes.
5. Shelters out of palm leaves.

PAGE 7

1. Fish was covered in salt and dried in the sun.
2. Hide-and-seek, hopscotch, blind man's buff, tug-of-war.
3. Farmers and traders.
4. Paved roads.
5. Battering rams.

PAGE 9

1. Tents and wineskins.
2. Swaddling clothes.
3. The skins were soaked in water with leaves, oil and bark.
4. Murex shellfish.
5. A shield and armor: a metal helmet and breastplate. Army commanders also wore grieves.

PAGE 10

1. On the walls of a hot clay oven.
2. Unleavened bread, roast lamb and bitter herbs.
3. Donkeys, mules and camels.
4. Leopards, foxes, jackals, hyenas and wild dogs.
5. Cumin, dill, cinnamon and mint.
6. Feast of Tabernacles.

PAGE 13

1. Barley and wheat.
2. Sheep and goats.
3. Passover, Pentecost and Tabernacles.
4. Grapes, dates, figs, mulberries, pomegranates, carob beans, nuts and olives.
5. Merchants from Africa and Arabia.

PAGE 15

1. On a simple loom at home.
2. Food, drink and somewhere to stay.
3. Over an open fire or in a small oven.
4. Reading, writing, numeracy and the religious law.
5. Carpenters, potters, metal-workers

PAGE 17

1. The Fish Gate, the Sheep Gate and the "Tower of the Ovens".
2. People squelched the grapes with their feet.
3. Carpenters.
4. Pipes were made from reeds; horns from animals' horns.

PAGE 19

1. In the spring.
2. Oxen.
3. White.
4. The Sabbath: Friday evening to Saturday evening.
5. Swords, spears, javelins, daggers and arrows.

PAGE 21

1. Nineveh in Babylon.
2. Wash their feet.
3. Carpenters.
4. Cranes, storks, swallows and quails.
5. Baal and Astarte.

PAGE 22

1. A sling.
2. Cooking, lighting and as a medicine.
3. Zacchaeus.
4. Monkeys and peacocks.
5. Solomon's Temple.

PAGE 25

1. Zerubbabel.
2. Thirteen.
3. Burial places.
4. Metal-workers.
5. Lebanon.

PAGE 27

1. Two.
2. Herod the Great.
3. Iron.
4. The Persians.
5. Horses.

Published in the United States of America by Abingdon Press, 201 Eighth Avenue South, Nashville, TN 37203, USA

ISBN 0 687 02654 7

First edition 2003

British Library Cataloguing in Publication Data. A catalogue record for this book is available from the British Library.

Printed and bound in Malaysia.